,

You are ...

Never Unloved

God loves you with an Unconditional,
unending, everlasting love.

Live Loved !

♡ *Lisa Dorr*

* * * * * * *
~ ~ ~ ~ ~ ~

Cover Design by Josh Dorr

Dedication

This book is dedicated to Caleb
Michael Shuff who, at three or four
years old, yelled to me across his
yard as I was leaving after a fun
time of playing together with him
and his sisters, the truth that will
forever be in my heart from him,
and a Truth from the Lord Jesus
Christ for all who choose to believe
that we are to,

"Always Remember To Never
Forget You Love Me."

Contents

Remember

"Do this in remembrance of me."
(Luke 22:19)

Paradise! What does that look like for you? For Adam and Eve, it was walking in the cool of the day with God in a meticulously manicured garden. One so beautiful, they need only to enjoy. It was created for their pleasure. They could walk hand-in-hand with each other, because their hands did not need to toil the land. Sure they had work to do, but it wasn't hard work.

Even their grooming of the Garden was enjoyable. God had given them everything for life and godliness. Perfectly loved by the Almighty God; His creation was created for them. What else could they possible want? It was paradise. It was *their* Paradise!

Perfectly placed in the middle of their Paradise were two trees. Both so breathtakingly gorgeous. Both so tempting. One given to them freely as part of their package to enjoy. The other totally forbidden. Wait. What? Did you just hear the sound track come to a screeching halt? Why in the world, in *this* world —in Adam and Eve's Paradise— would anything be off limits— totally forbidden? Weren't all things to be enjoyed? And such a strong word…forbidden!

Choices. We all have them. In the beginning, when God created everything, the choices for Adam and Eve might have been which path they should leisurely stroll along and enjoy for the day, what conversation could they have with God, or what delicious fruit would they sink their

perfectly, strong, white teeth into.
Now, this forbidden tree was
jamming up the works. Well, it
wasn't actually the tree itself. They
loved God so much and were so
grateful for all He'd given them;
they loved His presence and were
completely and utterly in love with
one another. It was actually easy to
obey God. The tree wasn't a
distraction. God commanded them
not to eat of that tree and it was
settled in their hearts. He said it,
they would obey it. Done. Or was it?
Would they obey or would they be
deceived? Deceived? Deceived by

whom? Out of their great love for God, they wanted to obey. So what happened? Did something or someone deceive them?

Along comes a slithering snake. Some people like snakes. I don't understand that, because I do not like them. I'm not necessarily afraid of them. I just don't like them. Well, just like the tree itself wasn't the problem, the snake in and of itself wasn't the problem either. It was the lie! The lie was the problem. What lie? Well, actually, the problem wasn't even the lie. It was that Adam and Eve needed to remember what God had said. Did they forget? Do we forget? God very clearly said to Adam, "You are free to eat from any tree in the garden; but you must not eat from the tree of the knowledge of good and evil, for when you eat of it you will surely die" (Genesis 2:17). In my Bible, the line just above this one says, "And the LORD God *commanded* the man" (Genesis 2:16, emphasis mine). God wasn't messing around. He was serious. He said it. Commanded it. But if you look more closely with me, He didn't expect Adam, or the woman He created for him, to obey because we see one little word that tells us God knew they would eat of this tree. Now, we could get all hung up on translation and versions. One version of the Bible says one thing and another one says something else. I don't get distracted by that because God led me to the NIV version of the Bible, I sense His presence when I read it; I believe He is talking to me, and I receive from Him. He tells us His Word is alive and active. I choose to believe it. But I'm getting ahead of myself. What word did God use that has us thinking God knew Adam and Eve would not obey His command? Well, it's right there. Not in His warning to not eat of the tree, but in His explanation of what would happen w.h.e.n. they would eat of the tree. "For *when* you eat of it you will surely die" (Genesis 2:17, emphasis mine).

God knows everything! He created everything! He had and has a plan. A plan that includes you and me—everyone. From the book of Genesis through to the end of the book of Revelation, we get to look more closely into God's perfect plan. We get to learn of God's character and His great plan for His creation. Not just for Adam and Eve and their beautiful Garden, but a plan for us and the beautiful life He has here on earth for us and eternally with Him in Heaven. He has planned it all out, yes, for you and me, and for everyone. Will you journey through the Bible to learn what He has said, what He's saying to you today? We first need to know what God said. Then we need to choose to obey. And after that, we need to always remember and never forget.

Could it have gone smoothly for Adam and Eve, where there would have been no sin, no death, no separation from God? Could Adam and Eve have just enjoyed God's presence and obeyed His command? Could they have lived in their Paradise forever—together, hand-in-hand, in the cool of the day, enjoying one another, God's creation, and the Presence of God daily? Could we?

~~*~*~*~*~*

What is it God said in His Word, that
we need to know?

"For God so loved the world that he
gave
his one and only Son,
that whoever believes in him
shall not perish but have eternal
life."
(John 3:16)

~~*~*~*~*~*

Remember, God had a plan, and He had His plan in motion for you and for me—for everyone, before Adam and Eve ate from The Tree of the Knowledge of Good and Evil. That was revealed as we read the word *when,* "when you eat of it you will surely die." But we read on and we see Adam and Eve live, they are banished from the Garden, they have Cain and Able, and their story continues. They did not die physically, but worse; they died spiritually. The death they experienced was a death of the relationship they had with God.

They disobeyed God—they sinned —and their sin now separated them from God. They were banished from the Garden because God's great plan was to reconcile us to Himself by giving His One and Only Son....

Had God allowed them to stay in the Garden and eat from the other tree, The Tree of Life, they would have stayed in their sinful state forever. But the giving that God did of His One and Only Son was for them to be brought back into right relationship with Himself. He loved Adam and Eve, and all His creation to come, too much to have us all separated from Him.

What does it mean when we read the words "he gave"? The giving of His Son is a gift to us. When we're given a gift, we can choose to open it and enjoy it. We can choose to open it and not enjoy it. Or, we can choose to not open it —sometimes not for a very long time—sometimes never. But God wants you and I to know, we are never unloved. Not then, not now, not ever. "For God so *loved* the world that he gave…" and He gave

His best! He gave His One and Only Son. This is Truth we need to know.

Since sin separated Adam and Eve from God w.h.e.n. they ate from The Tree of the Knowledge of Good and Evil after God had told them not to do that, and God loved them so much, He allowed much to happen in the world before He revealed His great plan. Never, not once, though, through it all, do we see God not loving them. Not *tolerating* the sin, yes! But always loving Adam and Eve. Loving us too. And, loving us so much that we are the ones who benefit from Adam and Eve's sin. Yes, we benefit! God knew they would sin and it would affect us down through the generational line. Some people don't want to be "blamed" for Adam and Eve's sin. They're not. They are "blamed" for their own sin that they did, whatever it was, because they made the choice to do whatever that behavior of sin was. It is, however, because of Adam and Eve that we got the sinful nature, which caused us to make the choice to sin. But, when we look at God's goodness, we see that because He knew this would happen, He made His plan that included us so we, too, would not be separated from Him, but be put back in right relationship with Him through His Son and so we could *eat* from the other tree in the Garden, The Tree of Life, now a metaphor, then, a physical reality. God wants us to never have to die. But His One and Only Son had to die in order for us not to die. What's with all this dying? Why would anyone need to die? It's all because of the Law. When we look back at the Old Testament, we see that there were many, many laws—too many to keep and too hard to keep. But the Law showed us our transgression. The Law pointed out sin.

What is it God said in His Word, that we need to know?

"For all have sinned and fall short of
the glory of God,
and are justified freely by his
grace
through the redemption that came
by Christ Jesus."
(Romans 3:23-24)

~~*~*~*~*

"God presented Christ as a sacrifice of atonement, through the shedding of his blood—to be received by faith. He did this to demonstrate his righteousness, because in his forbearance he had left the sins committed beforehand unpunished—he did it to demonstrate his righteousness at the present time, so as to be just and the one who justifies those who have faith in Jesus" (Romans 3:25-26). Putting our faith in Jesus, is not just a good thing to choose to do, it is what gives us life—life eternal. It's what puts us back in right relationship with God. Sin separated us from God, and Jesus Christ's shed blood puts us back in right relationship with God. But what's the connection? It's in the atonement.

Now, there are many things we, I, will not be able to explain. Remember, we're asked to believe by faith. We have plenty of facts, Truths, realities to understand and embrace, but some things will need to be believed by faith, and it's our choice to believe or not.

It is as simple as acknowledging the Truths spoken of above: that we are a sinner, in need of a savior, believing that Jesus Christ, God's One and Only Son is that Savior, asking Him to forgive our sin and put us back in right relationship with Him as we believe by faith that Jesus died in our place, making atonement for our sinful nature. As we make that exchange, through prayer—our sinful nature— for Christ's righteous nature—we receive God's free gift of salvation given to us to enjoy our new nature! This puts us back in right relationship with God. We are forgiven of our sin—past, present, and future—sin. We can enjoy a loving relationship with God through His Son Jesus Christ here on earth and eternally in Heaven.

I will be eternally grateful for making that choice and receiving God's free gift of salvation, as I made that exchange with God, through prayer, December 4th, 1991, and became a new creation in Christ. I am no longer a sinner; I am a saint. I no longer have a sinful nature; I have a righteous nature. I enjoy a

loving relationship with God
through His Son, Jesus Christ
because I believe by faith that His
blood shed on the cross made
atonement for my sin—past, present,
and future—sin. I am enjoying my
gift. I chose to *open* it and *enjoy* it.
Have you? It's available to you.
God's great plan set in motion
w.h.e.n. Adam and Eve were
choosing to disobey God and eat
from that tree included you. God
thought of you then, He's thinking
of you now. You are never unloved.

New Nature

"Therefore,
if anyone is in Christ, he is a new
creation;
the old has gone, the new has
come!"
(2 Corinthians 5:17)

Have you ever noticed that
sometimes people mix up the
meanings of words? I know I have.
I've noticed and I've mixed them up
myself. Sometimes it's done
negatively. The word I'm thinking
about is Holy. It means set apart, but
sometimes, negatively, people think
when Christians are referred to as

Holy that we are saying we are better than everyone else, or we think we are. Not true. Another word misunderstood and misused is saint. When I said earlier I am no longer a sinner, but now, because I put my faith in Jesus Christ as my Savior and through prayer I made the exchange on the cross—my sinful nature—for Christ's righteous nature, I am now a saint; I am not saying I am perfect. That's the negative way people think we Christians are saying we're a saint. The truth is, no one will be perfect until we are in Heaven, because this side of Heaven we will be tempted by satan to sin like everyone else, sometimes, daily. And, by the way, the word perfect is sometimes misunderstood and misused, too. It means complete.

Why do I then refer to myself as a saint? Because that is my new nature. I can no longer be the same if I accepted God's free gift. I am now a new creation in Christ. But you might argue that I still sin. Well, hopefully not intentionally or habitually, but yes, I am tempted by the enemy to sin. I, however, have the same power God used to raise Jesus from the dead living inside me. And that power and my love for Jesus helps me choose not to sin.

~~*~*~*~*~*

What is it God said in His Word, that we need to know?

"He predestined us for adoption to sonship through Jesus Christ, in accordance with his pleasure and will."
(Ephesians 1:5)

~~*~*~*~*~*

When you and I were created by God, we were created in His image. But because of the sin that took place in the Garden between Adam and Eve, we now live in a fallen world, a sin-separating-from-God-world. Well, God loved us too much to stay separated from us. He put His plan in motion by sending Jesus to this earth to redeem us. Jesus was the One and Only perfect/complete, spotless Lamb, the sacrifice acceptable to God according to The Law to cleanse our sin. Ok, if you're thinking, *what are you talking about*? Please allow me to explain. It's really not that difficult to understand, but we do get caught up in trying to use too many words to explain that God loved us, sin separated us, Jesus atoned for us, and God adopted us. We are now children of God. In the book of Revelation in the Bible, God says Jesus is knocking on the door of our hearts. If we open that door and let Him in, He will come in and once He's in, unless we kick Him out, He's here to stay. We are family. We can no longer *not* be family. We can choose to do wrong and have bad

behavior, but we're still family.
We're God's child. We're His.

What is it God said in His Word, that
we need to know?

"Never will I leave you;
never will I forsake you."
(Hebrews 13:5)

If you've made that exchange with Jesus, and I hope you have, then you are adopted into God's family and all God's Promises for you, His child, are now *yes* and *amen*. Here's another word people sometimes misunderstand or misuse and that is, amen. It means, so be it. Sometimes people think it means The End. Like the end of a prayer. When we say, "amen," we are agreeing with what's been prayed and saying, "so be it."

Having a new nature and having been adopted as God's child,

puts us in the family of God and we will forever have God with us. If you are in the family of God, your past has no hold on you. Hopefully you are so free that when you think of your past or it is brought up by someone else, you're able to think as though it were someone else—because it is. It's no longer you who lives, but Christ who lives in you.

You have crucified that old man, sinful nature, with Christ. When you are baptized in water, after making the decision to put your faith in Jesus and His atoning work done on the cross, you solidify the death-to-life experience by *drowning* that old man. Or at least you have the event to remember, praise God for it, and, also, to remind the enemy when he brings up your past. You can simply say, "that is no longer me; it is no longer a part of my nature. I am free!"

~~*~*~*~*~*

What is it God said in His Word, that
we need to know?

"Do not conform any longer
to the pattern
of this world,
but be transformed by the renewing
of your mind."
(Romans 12:2)

~~*~*~*~*~*

If we are going to follow Jesus
and His ways, we need to have the
mind of Christ. He tells us His
thoughts and His ways are higher
than ours, but we need to read the

Bible and allow His ways to change us by thinking differently. When we read what He says about us, we must believe what He's said. If we need help believing Him, we just have to ask Him. He's a Father who knows how to give good gifts to His children. He wants us free from the things we believed about ourselves before the great exchange, things others said about us, and things we've said about ourselves. We need to believe His Truth. He's given us His Name. The Name that is above all other names. The Name that has the power to redeem, heal, restore, and yes, transform our thinking. So, what's in a name? Often in the Bible God changed the name of an individual when they were transformed. Like Abram, who became Abraham, and Sari, who became Sarah, and Saul, who became Paul.

Authority

"All authority in heaven and on
earth
has been given to me."
(Matthew 28:18)

When you and I are issued a
credit card, our names are put on
that card. We can issue other family
members to have the same card and
have their name on that card, too.
Anyone who's name is on that credit
card has the authority to purchase
things with that card. Other people,
whose names are not on that card,

however, do not have the authority to use it.

Jesus purchased us with His blood. He shed His blood on the cross, paying the debt for our sin. You and I owed a debt we could not pay and Jesus paid a debt He did not owe.

~~*~*~*~*~*

What is it God said in His Word, that

we need to know?

"For the wages of sin is death,
but the gift of God is eternal life
in Christ Jesus our Lord."
(Romans 6:23)

~~*~*~*~*~*

Our names are written in the

Lambs Book of Life. Sealed. We

now have the authority to use Jesus'

name and ask Him for anything.

That's why we end our prayers, "In

Jesus' name, amen." We are saying,

"by the authority given to me in Jesus, so be it." It's also why we can make good choices when, even as a new creation, we are tempted to sin. We have the same power living inside us that God used to raise Jesus from the dead. The power of God! Living inside us! Accepting by faith that Jesus' blood atoned for our sin, we pray and ask Jesus into our hearts; we've opened that door He was knocking on that we read about in the book of Revelation, and we invited Him in. And because we did, He lives inside us.

One of the things I love the most about my relationship with God is that I am never alone. The Holy Spirit lives inside me and has promised to never *not* live there. Do you see why the words spoken to me by sweet, little Caleb are so precious and so powerful? We are to always remember and not forget that God promised to always live inside us once we've asked Him to do so.

~~*~*~*~*~*

What is it God said in His Word, that
we need to know?

"You will receive power
when the Holy Spirit comes on
you."
(Acts 1:8)

~~*~*~*~*~*

This power spoken of in Acts is
a result of Jesus ascending into
Heaven and leaving His Holy Spirit
to live inside believers. As a
believer, you've confessed your sin,
accepted by faith Jesus' removal of

that sinful nature and replacement of Christ's righteous nature, so you have a nice tidy place—your heart— for the Holy Spirit to live. Now when the accuser of the brethren, satan, comes to tempt you and I, we can recognize him and tell him to GO! James 4:7 says, "Submit yourselves, then, to God. Resist the devil, and he will flee from you." With the authority you and I have in the shed blood of Jesus Christ and the Holy Spirit's power living inside us, we do not have to succumb to the enemy's attacks. He will continually try, but we are over-comers.

Scripture tells us in Revelation 12:11 that, "They triumphed over him by the blood of the Lamb and by the word of their testimony." So, sin no longer lives in our hearts; we have everything we need for life and godliness. Where have we heard that before? Now, living as a new creation, with the authority given to us in Jesus, and the power of the Holy Spirit inside us, this is as close to *paradise* as we will get this side of Heaven. It's not Adam and Eve's Paradise; it's our *paradise*—yours, mine, and every believer's *paradise*. All because of God's great love.

Break [It] OFF

"Do not conform any longer
to the pattern of
this world,
but be transformed by the renewing
of your mind."
(Romans 12:2)

Keeping a clean heart for the Holy Spirit to feel comfortable living in is our daily challenge. We need to read God's Word every day in order to know what He is saying to us and to allow Him to continually be renewing our minds. When we come to faith in Christ, we come with baggage and bondage.

All of that is crucified with Christ and left at the foot of the cross. We don't need to carry it any longer. But sometimes we do carry it. Our mind needs to be transformed. We need to know what God says about us and we need to believe it. This is called a walk. It's a journey, a life-long-journey, walking with Jesus.

One of the things that helped me so much with this when I first came to know Jesus as my Savior, was a book called *The Bondage Breaker* by Neil Anderson. By reading, praying, and practically devouring, the Scriptures he listed, I was able to change the thoughts I had about myself, and thoughts of words spoken to me and about me, with the Truth of God's Word and what God said about me. And then believe it! Lauren Daigle's song, "You Say," says it clearly—I Believe.

In Neil Anderson's book, *The Bondage Breaker*, he helps the believer go back through generational things, and break off, through prayer and acknowledging the blood line now drawn between that time or incident, anything and everything, that was attached to you before you surrendered your life to Christ. We are all just history-repeating-beings until we give our lives to Jesus. Going through the steps in his book helped me to tell the enemy, he no longer had access to [it] in my life, and, also, helped me acknowledge that [it] was under the blood. What is the [it] in your life, or many [its], that the enemy needs to know he no longer has access to, and, you, need to acknowledge that Jesus' blood covered? It's a simple thing, but a very powerful thing. It's simple because we all have a past; we have generational things passed down to us, and it is powerful because that's where God comes in and takes [it] away—forever!

~~*~*~*~*~*

What is it God said in His Word, that we need to know?

"As far as the east is from the west, so far has he removed our transgressions from us."
(Psalm 103:12)

~~*~*~*~*~*

If something has been broken off you and I, through prayer, then it no longer is part of us. We can now walk in that freedom. Remember, we're walking with Jesus daily. We're reading our Bibles and learning about God and His ways, and with the power of the Holy Spirit living inside us, when our desires align with God's desires, we are becoming more and more like Jesus.

Sometime ago there was a movement where the letters W.W.J.D. were on bracelets and tee shirts and all kinds of things, mugs, you name it, those letters were everywhere. In my opinion it was a great movement and one we would do well to reinstate. The letters stand for What. Would. Jesus. Do. When we stopped what we were doing, or we stopped what we were saying, and asked, "What Would Jesus Do?" we had an opportunity to do and say what He would do and say. Wow! What a way to live?!

Neil Anderson's book has a list of Scriptures in the back of his book. The list starts out with the words, In

Christ… so, these scriptures are for the believer. Remember, your name needs to be on the credit card in order to have the authority to access it. So, these Promises are for the believer because our names are written in the Lamb's Book of Life. Here are some that have helped over the years to transform my thinking:

In Christ…

I Am Significant:

Matthew 5:13   I am the salt of the
                earth.

Matthew 5:14   I am the light of the
                world.

John 1:12   I am God's child

John 15:1, 5   I am a branch of the
                true vine, a channel
                of His life.

John 15:16   I have been chosen
                and appointed to
                bear fruit.

Acts 1:8	I am a personal witness of Christ's.
1 Cor. 3:16	I am God's temple.
1 Cor. 12:27	I am a member of Christ's body.
Eph. 1:1	I am a saint

In Christ...

I Am Accepted:

John 15:15   I am Christ's friend.

1 Cor. 6:20   I have been bought
with a price. I
belong to God.

2 Cor. 5:21   I have been made
righteous.

Eph. 2:19   I am a fellow citizen
with the rest of the
saints.

Col. 2:10   I am complete in
Christ.

In Christ…

I Am Secure:

John 1:12   I am a child of God.

Rom. 8:35   I cannot be separated
                from the love of
                God.

Rom. 8:1   I am free forever
                from condemnation.

Eph. 1:13, 14   I have been given
                the Holy Spirit as a
                pledge, guaranteeing
                my inheritance to
                come.

Col. 1:13   I have been
delivered from the
domain of darkness
and transferred to
the kingdom of
Christ.

Phil. 1:6   I am confident that
the good work that
God has begun in
me will be perfected.

Do you recognize some of the words we talked about in other chapters? These are all things God said in His Word, that we need to know. I read, and still read, these Scriptures over and over and over, again, to transform my mind and help me believe what God has already said about me. I hope you'll read these, too, and have your mind transformed, because as a believer, God has said these things about you, too. It's Truth—True Truth. I call these Scriptures my, "I Am Scriptures" because they tell me who I am In Christ. And, I choose to believe by faith. I hope you will allow the Holy Spirit to reveal to you what needs broken off you and, through prayer, just do it! Believe the Truth about what the Almighty God says about you and walk in the freedom of who you used to be.

What is it God said in His Word, that we need to know?

"So if the Son sets you free,
you will be free indeed."
(John 8:36)

~~*~*~*~*~*

Today is your day to break off old, dead, things keeping you in bondage. Break [It] Off! In the name of Jesus. The most powerful Name there is. The Name which was given to you as you acknowledged you were a sinner in need of a savior and, through faith, accepted the work done on the cross by Jesus; you became a new creation In Christ. It is no longer you who lives, but Christ who lives within you. So, believe you are free, because you are —you are free indeed.

You will look more like Jesus, talk more like Jesus, and if you want to get the bracelet and the tee shirt, great! But, you already have everything you need for life and godliness. You just need to accept it, believe it, and walk in it. You, my dear sister or dear brother In Christ, are **Never Unloved**! You are to **Remember** what God said in His Word, so you can make that exchange with Jesus on the cross— your sinful nature—for His righteous nature, and become a **New Creation.** You have been given **Authority** to pray in Jesus' name and walk in freedom, as you **Break [It] Off**.

Embrace By Faith

"We live by faith, not by sight."
(2 Corinthians 5:7)

What would happen if you just disregarded all this Truth? All the things we've been talking about as a new creation that are yours In Christ Jesus? Sadly, many people do. And when we do, we live unproductive lives. We circle around the same issues and struggle unnecessarily. It doesn't have to be that hard.

~~*~*~*~*~*

What is it God said in His Word, that
we need to know?

"Whatever is true, whatever is
noble, whatever is right, whatever is
pure,
whatever is lovely,
whatever is admirable—if anything
is excellent
or praiseworthy—think about such
things."
(Philippians 4:8)

Many years ago, I read the book, *Telling Yourself The Truth,* by William Backus and Marie Chapian. When anxiety was raging and thoughts were out of control, this book helped settle that by asking the question, *what's the truth*? It could also be asked of us during a time of much stress, *what's the lie*? Just like when we first got saved and we needed to renew our minds by learning what God said about us, we need to continue reading His Word, the Bible, to know what He said, so we can believe it and walk in the Truth today.

We do live by faith, not by sight. But, it's not blind faith. It's faith in the Truth of God's Word. We have a choice—we always have a choice. And there are consequences to our choices. There are blessings in obedience. When we walk with God daily reading His Word and continually being transformed by it, we are blessed. Now, you may say, but there is still so much turmoil in my life and start naming the circumstances that are out of control.

~~*~*~*~*~*

What is it God said in His Word, that
we need to know?

"Praise be to the God and Father of
our Lord Jesus Christ,
who has blessed us in the heavenly
realms with
every spiritual blessing in Christ."
(Ephesians 1:3)

There was a time in my life
when I was super happy. Everything
seemed right in my paradise. I
thanked the LORD! But as I did, I
sensed in my spirit Him saying these

words to me, *I'm glad you're happy. But I have given you Every. Spiritual. Blessing. In Christ.* I didn't get it at first. I thought we were agreeing. I thought He was accepting my praise and my thanks for how happy I was, until I heard it again… *I'm glad you're happy. But I have given you Every. Spiritual. Blessing. In Christ.* Even now as I write this, familiar tears fill my eyes. Tears of joy. The depth of what God was saying to me was, and still is, so hard to comprehend. *Every. Spiritual. Blessing. In Christ.*

We can read the Bible and just blow past some of these deep Truths He's spoken, and is still speaking, to us. I just love it when He gets my attention, though, and I pause and receive what He is saying and embrace it. We've heard it said, and know it by experience, that you need to get close to someone to hear them whisper. It's like that with God, too. When we are close to Him He will whisper things to us, His children, to hear. Two Scriptures come to my mind and they are, "Be still, and know that I am God" (Psalm 46:10). And, "but the LORD was not in the wind. After the wind there was an earthquake, but the LORD was not in the earthquake. After the earthquake came a fire, but the LORD was not in the fire. And after the fire came a gentle whisper" (1 Kings 19:11, 12). Spending time with anyone helps us get to know them better. It's the same way with God; as we spend time reading His Word and praying we get to know Him better. Then when He whispers we can know it's Him. He doesn't have to shout when our circumstances seem louder than we can bear.

The morning I felt super happy and was giving Him thanks, I was giving Him thanks for my circumstances. He was taking me higher! Through Scripture, He was laying a foundation of my identity In Him to help me know when *wind* is blowing me here and there, and an *earthquake* of bad news tries to shatter my paradise, and a *fire* comes to burn up everything I thought was good, lovely, and pure, I can remember and embrace by faith the Truth He's already spoken to me in Ephesians 1:3…the God and Father of our Lord Jesus Christ has blessed me with *every spiritual blessing In Christ.*

Dear sister or brother In Christ, God loves us so very much that He has gone before us to lay a foundation that will hold us steady when life hits us. Did you catch that —w.h.e.n. life hits us. None of us is exempt. Now, before we get all doom and gloom here, we just need to know this as a fact of life. Remember, we live in a fallen world. We were made new, but our world was not. That's why when you hear the question asked, "why do

bad things happen to good people?",
or maybe you've asked that question
yourself, you can look to God and
His Promises and know that He
wants to take your thoughts higher
than your circumstances.

What if you're in that perfect
storm right now? The winds are
blowing, your paradise has been
shattered by what feels like an
earthquake, and the fire is raging so
fiercely out of control that you're
certain it will burn up everything
you've ever known and loved.
Embrace by faith dear one, all of

God's Promises for you, get close to Him like never before. In our house we have a saying and it goes like this, "Always run to God, never from Him." We adopted this saying at a time we felt the storm hitting us would take us under. We clung to God, His Promises, and to each other. God is for you, not against you. You will get through this. And, God will work good out of it. He is our defender, our redeemer, our God in whom we can trust. Nothing is a surprise to Him. Trust Him today, and embrace by faith what He's telling you. He's the same God yesterday, today, and forever. May we sing, "It Is Well With My Soul," in the good times and the bad times, because He doesn't change. Sometimes in life we have to walk by faith, not by sight. But oh, the reward we will have when we see Him face to face and we see the work He was doing behind the scenes to weave that beautiful tapestry of our lives into the beautiful picture He can already see. While we're embracing by faith, He is seeing clearly.

Community

"He who walks with the wise grows
wise,
but a companion of fools suffers
harm."
(Proverbs 13:20)

We had each other (my
"Hubbin" and son and I) when we
were going through a storm. And,
we had many wonderful friends,
pastors, and a counselor. We were
never meant to do life alone. We
need community. Everyone was very
helpful as they prayed for us and
encouraged us. We got through it,
and you will too.

If you know me, you've heard me say that my individual girlfriends are like flowers—each one beautiful and unique—and all together they make a beautiful bouquet. We're all created by God and we are created in His image. He is The Creator. He's made each one of us a little different from the other. He's given us different gifts to use and enjoy and be enjoyed by others. We have each other to encourage, bless, and do life with. Whatever you call it: Life Group, Small Group, Cell Group—just have a group. Do life with others. You may just be who someone else is looking for. Is it that easy? Sure it is. It's God's will for you and I to be in community, so it aligns with what He wants for us.

What is it God said in His Word, that we need to know?

"The body is a unit,
though it is made up of many parts;
and though all its parts are many,
they all form one body. So it is with
Christ."
(1 Corinthians 12:12)

~~*~*~*~*~*

Being the body of Christ is such an awesome privilege. If you've ever felt like you don't belong, remember to embrace Truth. God is telling us we belong and we are His hands and feet. Of course, the body is made up of many parts and each one is very important. It all functions together. Or it should. That's the way God intended it to be.

My sweet friend, Tabitha Deller, is one of those *flowers* I've referred to. She blesses me, encourages me, and we "get to" do life together. She is the author of *Called, Brave,* and *Near.* In her book, *Called,* she writes in the chapter *Called To Need...*

I believe our needs are twofold and can be met in different ways. First of all, and probably the easiest, most natural, and the way we gravitate to have our needs met the most is through each other. People are tangible. They talk back to us. They give us advice, and they can physically meet a need we may have in a moment's notice. God's word in Romans 12:13 says, "Share

with the Lord's people who are in
need. Practice hospitality." We read
again in Hebrews 10:25 that we
should "not give up meeting
together, as some are in the habit of
doing, but encouraging one
another." We all know that a
recurring theme in God's word is
sacrificial love and giving—
modeling what Christ did for us. We
are challenged to honor one another
above ourselves in Romans 12:10.
He uses others in our lives and
desires to use us in the lives of
others to be His hands and feet.
Although others are meeting the

need, He always remains the source of the blessing.

What is it God said in His Word, that we need to know?

"Though one may be overpowered,
two can defend themselves.
A cord of three strands is not
quickly broken."
(Ecclesiastes 4:12)

People are important. God promotes community. So, being connected with like-minded people brings a wholeness to us. We are not to be, "yoked together with unbelievers," God says, in 2 Corinthians 6:14. And He goes on to say, "For what do righteousness and wickedness have in common? Or what fellowship can light have with darkness?" Have you heard the analogy of the clean rag/dirty rag? It goes like this: if you put a clean rag together with a dirty rag, is the dirty rag going to get clean or is the clean rag going to get dirty? We all know the answer is that the clean rag is going to get dirty. Now, this does not mean we are not to associate with unbelievers. God told us to, "Go into all the world and preach the good news to all creation" (Mark 16:15). But it does mean, as a believer, we do not marry an unbeliever, or be tied to an unbeliever in the way the three cords are spoken of in the above Scripture.

It's the word *yoke* that says it all. When we know that a yoke is what is put around two oxen to plow a field, we know that they cannot separate from each other. If one leads, the other must follow. So if the two *yoked* together are believers, and they are following Jesus and His ways, they will be blessed and encouraged and "get to" do life together in a way that pleases God.

One of my other *flowers* is my precious Rachel Inouye. The Holy Spirit alive in her is contagious! When she speaks at conferences and retreats, she's been known to say that it's as if she's been plugged into an electric socket and she is **On**. In reality she is plugged into the energy source—The Holy Spirit. She's grounded in God's Word and the Truth just spills out of her. Rachel is the author of *Lily Pads, He Speaks, I'm Listening, and Be-loved.* In her book, *He Speaks*, she journals things God has spoken to her and encourages you to listen for God's voice, too. She gives place inside her book to journal as you are cultivating the voice of God in your life. On the cover of her book she has pictures of many of her journals opened to her writing:

The Lord Says My Daughter, My Love...

We are His daughters. And if you're male then you are His son. He's speaking to us. He wants us to be yoked together with Him and listen to His voice. He wants to guide our steps and lead us in the righteous paths we should go. We "get to" follow Him and do life with Him and the lovely *flowers* He brings into our lives.

Live Loved

"I remain confident of this:
I will see the goodness of the LORD
in the land of the living."
(Psalm 27:13)

If you've picked up on the
words I've used, which show we
have a choice, the words "get to,"
you see that it is all about
perspective. We could say, "have
to," or "want to," or, even, "need
to." But I choose the words, "get to"
because I feel so very blessed.

We're in the last chapter of this
book and this is where we get to

choose if we'll remember the things God has said by reading His Word and allowing it to penetrate our hearts, where we would actually live out this great love God has provided for us. We have a choice to acknowledge we are a sinner in need of a savior and believe that Jesus Christ is that Savior. We have a choice to accept that His blood covered over our sin when it was shed on the cross and believe that we can become a new creation by exchanging our sinfulness for His righteousness. We have a choice to stand in the authority He has given us to stand in and fight the enemy, to believe we have everything we need In Christ. We have a choice to break it off, whatever that [it] is. We have a choice to embrace by faith. All these things take faith to believe—we have that choice! We have a choice to be in community and be yoked together with believers, and we have a choice to live loved. God has given us one life.

~~*~*~*~*~*

What is it God said in His Word, that
we need to know?

"I have come that they may have
life,
and have it to the full."
(John 10:10)

~~*~*~*~*~*

The writing of this book, *Never
Unloved*, came about as I was
reading one of Max Lucado's books,
Come Thirsty. I was open to writing
another book and three different

people at different times had encouraged me to do so. It wasn't until the words, *never unloved*, almost jumped off the page at me, that I knew this would be the title of my next book. The Holy Spirit very quickly impressed upon my heart that there were to be seven chapters; He gave me the titles, the order of the titles, the Scripture that was to go with each chapter, and from there I knew I would obey Him and write this book. It all came together very quickly and very easily because these are all things I embrace by faith. They are things that I have experienced and that I walk in daily with confidence. I hope it encourages you and equips you, my dear reader friend.

Each step of the process of writing came to me as the LORD led. The last part of it just came today as I began to finish the last two chapters.

~~*~*~*~*~*

What is it God said in His Word, that
we need to know?

"And my God will meet all your
needs
according to his glorious riches in
Christ Jesus"
(Philippians 4:19)

~~*~*~*~*~*

The Apostle Paul said in Philippians 4:12, "I know what it is to be in need, and I know what it is to have plenty. I have learned the secret of being content in any and every situation, whether well fed or hungry, whether living in plenty or in want. I can do everything through him who gives me strength." When we rely on God the way Paul did, we can have this contentment he spoke of. We can trust God will meet all our needs. And because He is such a good, good God, He often goes over and above. My very favorite Scripture is Ephesians 3:20, where

He says, "Now to him who is able to do immeasurably more than all we ask or imagine, according to his power that is at work within us, to him be glory in the church and in Christ Jesus throughout all generations, for ever and ever! Amen."

This is why we can trust that we will see the goodness of our God in the land of the living. Our relationship with the LORD Jesus Christ expands time. His love for us is for us to enjoy now, because of what He did on the cross, and it is for eternity—an amount of time we can not comprehend. We know love here on earth through people, we can trust and embrace by faith God's great love for us and believe in our hearts that we always were, and, will always be, loved by the Almighty God.

~~*~*~*~*~*

What is it God said in His Word, that
we need to know?

"For I am convinced that neither
death nor life,
neither angels nor demons,
neither the present nor the future,
nor powers,
neither height nor depth,
nor anything else in all creation,
will be able to separate us
from the love of God
that is in Christ Jesus our Lord."
(Romans 8:38, 39)

~~*~*~*~*~*

After I wrote down, as quickly as I could, all that I was hearing God say to me about writing my next book that day, I continued reading Max Lucado's book, *Come Thirsty*. As a directive from him to write a letter to the LORD, I took the challenge and wrote in my journal:

I want you to know LORD —I LOVE YOU! Just like your love for me is steadfast, I believe you would agree that mine has been steadfast, unwavering, since December 4th, 1991, when I learned I was a sinner in need of a savior *and <u>YOU</u> were that Savior. Going down under that water in the bathtub as the pastor prayed over me and baptized me, was the solidifying factor. The power and love I felt that day changed me forever! I've been on a continual quest for more of you, and for me to show my love to you more through my obedience to you. I LOVE YOUR WORD! The Bible is fresh air/ oxygen to me—Living Water— whatever analogy or metaphor best describes it.*

It is Everything to me, because you are everything to me. You are the Word. When I read the Word I am spending time with you. You are teaching me so much and I never want to stop learning. I want to influence others for you more than I do. I want to partner with you and love on others with your love. Please show me how best to do that. I think the thing I've been most tripped up with over the years is wanting more for someone than they want for themselves. I want all to come to the knowledge of your saving grace and live in freedom—live loved. Please

help me to know—not just know,
trust—not just trust, live—live out
the knowing and the trusting that
You Do The Work. Exodus 14:14 is
one of my favorites for a reason. You
use it to remind me, "The LORD will
fight for you; you need only to be
still." Wow, how I love you!

Thank you for EVERYthing.
You are amazing! I love you so very
much. I love being Yours. I love
knowing I'll always be yours.
Nothing can or will EVER separate
us. EVER! It's such an awesome
feeling to know I'm loved by The

Almighty God—The God of the universe. Thank you for loving me. Thank you that because of your great love for me—your un-ending, un-conditional, ever-lasting—love, I can, and do, Live Loved.

~ Notes ~

Chapter 4 — Break [It] Off

1. Neil T. Anderson, *The Bondage Breaker* (Eugene, Oregon: Harvest House Publishers, 1990/1993/2000), 55, 59, 61-65.

2. Lauren Daigle, "You Say" (*Look Up Child, 2018*), 55.

Chapter 6 — Community

1. Tabitha Deller, *Called* (Meadville, PA: Christian Faith Publishing, 2018), 89-91, *Brave*

(Monee, IL: 2020), *Near* (Middletown, DE: 2022), 89.

2. Rachel Inouye, *Lily Pads* (Charleston, SC: 2016)*, He Speaks, I'm Listening* (Monee, IL: 2020)*, Be-loved* (Kendaville, IN: 2022), 95-96.

Chapter 7 — Live Loved

1. Max Lucado, *Come Thirsty* (Nashville, Tennessee: W Publishing Group, a Division of Thomas Nelson, 2004), 100, 101, 108.

~ Resources ~

The Bondage Breaker: Overcoming Negative Thoughts Irrational Feelings Habitual Sins, by Neil T. Anderson (Eugene, Oregon: Harvest House Publishers, 1990/1993/2000).

Telling Yourself The Truth: Find Your Way Out of Depression, Anxiety, Fear, Anger and Other Common Problems by Applying Principles of Misbelief Therapy, by William Backus and Marie Chapian (Bloomington, Minnesota: Bethany House Publishers, 2014).

~Author Contact~

lisa.dorr.everylittledetail@gmail.com

http://lisaforhisglory.wixsite.com

~ About the Author ~

Still on a journey with the Lord Jesus Christ, Lisa Dorr lives her life yielded to the work of the Holy Spirit. She loves to encourage women to know who they are In Christ with Ephesians as her favorite book of the Bible. Blessed to have had opportunities to speak at MOPS and other Women's Ministry events, she has led Bible studies, worshiped on a worship team, is a contributing author and editor for *God Stories,* and has enjoyed writing *Every Little Detail* and *Daisy & Bee Scriptures and Devotionals for Today.* If you tune-in to WPFG 91.3 FM, it is likely you will hear her voice encouraging the listeners. She lives with her husband, son, and multiple cats in Dillsburg, Pennsylvania.

~Other Books by Lisa Dorr~

Every Little Detail
Find God in the details of
my story, your story,
and
His story

Daisy & Bee
*Scriptures and Devotionals for
Today*